GOD'S REVELATION TO THE HUMAN HEART

D1319533

God's Revelation to the Human Heart

Fr. Seraphim Rose

ST. HERMAN OF ALASKA BROTHERHOOD
2007

Copyright © 1987 by the
St. Herman of Alaska Brotherhood

First Printing, 1987
Second Printing, 1991
Third Printing, 1994
Fourth Printing, 1997
Fifth Printing, Second Edition, 2007

Address all correspondence to:
St. Herman of Alaska Brotherhood
P. O. Box 70
Platina, California 96076

www.sainthermanpress.com

Front cover: Fr. Seraphim in front of the Holy Doors at the
St. Herman Monastery, Platina, California, 1977.

ISBN-13: 978-0-938635-03-1
Library of Congress Control Number: 2007930305

CONTENTS

INTRODUCTION

by Hieromonk Damascene

In the spring of 1981, less than a year and a half before his repose, Fr. Seraphim Rose was invited to give a lecture at the University of California, Santa Cruz. His audience was to be comprised of students from a class on comparative religions, called "World Religions in the U.S."

Santa Cruz had been a center for the nationwide spiritual quest that had reached its peak in the late 1960s and early 1970s, and vestiges of this movement had continued into the 1980s. The young people who came to hear Fr. Seraphim's talk were representative of this quest, and had been traveling on a wide variety of spiritual paths. Popular in Santa Cruz at that time were various gurus who promised enlightenment or dazzled people with miracles: Rajneesh, Muktananda, Sri Chinmoy and numerous others who had achieved temporary fame. Many seekers at the university, bypassing the spiritual disciplines taught by the gurus, sought direct religious experience through hallucinogenic drugs. Still others, dissatisfied with the spiritual poverty of Western culture, sought higher reality in Tibetan and Zen Buddhism, or in modern reinventions of American Indian shamanism. Finally, there remained those who were seeking the truth in their Christian heritage. Western Christendom, however, had long since been cut off from the fulness of the Christian Faith: the fulness not only of ancient tradition and Divinely revealed wisdom, but also of the profound experience of God made possible by Christ in His

Church. Those who tried to make the best of contemporary Western Christianity, therefore, were prone to feel somewhat inferior before all the popularized religious traditions of the East, where the teachers had their metaphysics and mysticism up their shirt-sleeves, so to speak.

On May 15, 1981, Fr. Seraphim came before this gamut of spiritual currents with something different to say, something to which most of the people in his audience had never been exposed. He represented Christianity, the tradition that still influenced the whole of Western culture (whether consciously or unconsciously), and yet his was not the anemic, superficial American Christianity that so many seekers had left behind to look elsewhere. In his experience, he drew from the *full* revelation of Christ's truth, handed down by God-illumined teachers throughout the past twenty centuries. Christianity, he knew, had been "given a bad name" in the West; and yet how many honest searchers, if they knew all that it actually was, would not hesitate to embrace it?

Like the students whom he was addressing, Fr. Seraphim had once been an idealistic young American in search of the truth. Having rejected the Protestant religion of his formative years, he undertook a zealous study of East Asian wisdom, learning the language of ancient China in order to translate its religious texts. But the soul, as he later realized, naturally seeks a personal God; and thus he was led, almost in spite of himself, back to the all-compelling truth of Christ. Still, this conversion might have never taken place had he not discovered the Eastern Orthodox Church, which was all but unknown in Western society. This Church, he understood, was indeed the historical Church founded by Christ and His apostles, for it alone had retained the continuity and purity of ancient Christian teaching. However, it was not first of all the testimony of history that moved him to embrace the Orthodox Faith, since other religions can also claim faithfulness to their historical origins; rather, it was the fact that Orthodox Christianity alone satisfied his thirst for truth: it brought him into living communion with God through Divine grace, gave him a profound spiritual discipline in which he could grow into God's likeness, and at the same time provided him with the theological, metaphysical principles by which his penetrating mind could perceive the universe as a coherent whole, and the noble place of man within that whole.

Fr. Seraphim had devoted himself wholly to his search for truth, and when he found it he devoted himself no less fully to the service of it. Together with another Orthodox Christian of like mind, he began a missionary brotherhood, a bookstore and a periodical (*The Orthodox Word*) in San Francisco. Some years later, wishing to leave the tumult of the world and seek God in quiet seclusion, his brotherhood moved to the mountains of northern California, where it continued its missionary activity through the printed word. He spent the next thirteen years, the remainder of his short life, in this wilderness as a monk. An inward change was wrought in him during this time, as he became immersed in the Church's cycle and rhythm of prayers, and in the timeless writings of the Holy Fathers. By diligently studying Patristic texts with the purpose of practically using them for spiritual growth, he was able to think, feel and believe as the early Fathers had done, until at last he became as one of them: a Holy Father of modern times, one of the rare transmitters of unchanging Christian wisdom to the contemporary world.

Such was the calibre of the man who sat before the group

of students at the Santa Cruz university. With his piercing eyes, long beard and black robe, his appearance was as striking as that of the gurus to whom the young people were flocking. But his intention was not to impress them on such an external level: he knew that, for any of these students to come to the fulness of truth, something deeper would have to take place within them.

Fr. Seraphim was well aware of how spiritually insensitive modern man had become, and thus he knew that people often needed some supernatural "phenomena," some sensual but seemingly spiritual experiences, to awaken any response in them. That was why so many young seekers followed "holy men" or religious groups on the basis of the miracles they performed or the "results" they promised, as well as why hallucinogenic drugs, occult practices and so-called "charismatic" experiences had become so popular. Fr. Seraphim wished to tell the students that this desire to experience or see something "spiritual," something beyond mundane everyday life, was not the right reason to undertake a spiritual quest. If one is honest, one will seek nothing but the fulness of truth (as Fr. Seraphim himself had done), and will not stop at a state where only a portion of the truth is present, eliciting a deceptive feeling of satisfaction.

It is true that Fr. Seraphim had witnessed many miracles during his life. One of his mentors, Archbishop John Maximovitch,* had been a worker of wonders in the same way that the first apostles had been. Fr. Seraphim would tell the students of some of these wonders, but he would do this only

---

* Archbishop John was canonized by the Russian Orthodox Church Outside of Russia in 1994 as St. John of Shanghai and San Franscisco.

Fr. Seraphim on "Noble Ridge," in the wilderness surrounding the St. Herman of Alaska Monastery, Platina, California.

Fr. Seraphim's cabin in the mountains of northern California.

to lead them towards deeper considerations. His ultimate aim, of course, was to awaken people to that which they truly desired: the living Christ. He recognized that, for all the spiritual denseness of contemporary Western man, the basic process of his conversion was no different from what it had been in past ages. Conversion takes place when something in the heart is touched, when the heart begins to "burn" at being in contact with God-revealed truth. Before this can take place, however, the person often has to feel an absence of this truth, and to actually experience suffering as a result of this want. People in the affluent Western world often have this feeling of spiritual torment suppressed from their consciousness, so occupied are they with physical comforts and stimulations. In countries where people are deprived of freedom and comfort, on the other hand, the spiritual hunger of man becomes more immediate and desperate. Therefore, Fr. Seraphim realized, people in the free world have an important lesson to learn from those behind the iron curtain concerning the awakening of religious faith. But could the former people, living in what might be called a "fool's paradise," translate the real and essential experience of the latter into a form that they could even begin to understand? Fr. Seraphim hoped so, for he knew that, without a knowledge of Golgotha and the Cross, one could never come to a real knowledge of Christ the incarnate God, Who is *the Resurrection and the Life* (John 11:25).

One of Fr. Seraphim's intentions in speaking to the students was to show them that spiritual life was not just something to be "enjoyed," but was rather a kind of battleground where the soul becomes purified through suffering. To many of the students this was a novel concept; for who of the modern-day religious figures, wishing to gain a popular following, would have called people to a way of ceaseless suffering and struggle? Such, however, was the way that Christ Himself went and beckoned men to follow. And Fr. Seraphim, indicating this narrow path in the course of his lecture, moved some of his listeners to take up their crosses and follow it.

Unfortunately, judging from the questions he was asked after his lecture, the majority of the students seemed to somehow "miss the point." He had been speaking about the elemental reality of Christian life, what it means to be converted in one's heart and transformed by Christ. He had called the search for truth "a matter of life or death." In contrast to this urgency, many of the questions he was asked appeared to be motivated by little more than idle curiosity. He was put on the spot with questions about what he thought of various Christian bodies, about where he thought the Holy Spirit was and was not, about the "million and one little differences" between Orthodoxy and Roman Catholicism, etc.—as if his questioners were trying to "categorize" what he said rather than let themselves be moved by it. What is inspiring is that, even when he was compelled to answer these questions, he continued to speak *the truth in love,* as he had done during his lecture, and to draw people's minds towards a more spiritual way of understanding things.

Fr. Seraphim lecturing during the "New Valaam Theological Academy" courses, St. Herman of Alaska Monastery, Platina, California, 1980.

Photograph by Fr. Lawrence Williams.

God's Revelation
to the Human Heart

1. THE SEARCH

Why does a person study religion? There are many incidental reasons, but there is only one reason if a person is really in earnest: in a word, it is to come into contact with reality, to find a reality deeper than the everyday reality that so quickly changes, rots away, leaves nothing behind and offers no lasting happiness to the human soul. Every religion that is sincere tries to open up contact with this reality. I would like to say a few words today about how Orthodox Christianity tries to do this—to open up spiritual reality to the religious seeker.

The search for reality is a dangerous task. You all have probably heard stories of how young people in our times of searching have "burned themselves out" trying to find reality, and either die young or drag out a dreary existence at a fraction of their potential of mind and soul. I myself recall a friend from the days of my own searching twenty-five years ago, when Aldous Huxley had just discovered the supposedly "spiritual" value of LSD and had influenced many to follow him. This young man, a typical religious searcher who might be attending a course like this, once told me: "No matter what you might say of the dangers of drugs, you must admit that *anything* is better than everyday American life, which is spiritually dead." I disagreed, since even then I was beginning to glimpse that spiritual life spreads in two directions: it can lead one *higher* than this everyday life of corruption, but it can also lead one *lower* and bring about a literal spiritual—as well as physical—death. He went his own way, and before he was thirty years old he was a wreck of an old man, his mind ruined, and any search for reality abandoned.

Similar examples could be found among people who seek various forms of psychic experiences, experiment in "out-of-body" states, have encounters with UFOs, and the like. (The experience of the Jonestown mass-suicide in 1980 is enough to remind us of the dangers inherent in the religious search.) Our Orthodox literature over the past two thousand years has quite a few instructive examples of this sort. Here I will cite just one, from the life of St. Nicetas of the Kiev Caves, who lived nearly a thousand years ago in Russia:

> Drawn by zeal, Nicetas asked his Abbot to bless him to live in reclusion. The Abbot (who was then St. Nikon) forbade him, saying, "My son! It is not good for you who are young to be idle. Better for you to live with the brethren. By serving them you will not lose your reward. You know yourself how Isaac was deluded by demons in reclusion. He would have perished if the special grace of God, through the prayers of our holy Fathers Antony and Theodosius, had not saved him."
>
> "Father," Nicetas replied, "I will never be deceived by anything of that kind, but I want to stand firmly against the wiles of the demons and to ask God to give

me the gift of miracle-working, like Isaac the Recluse, who even till now performs many miracles."

"Your desire," said the Abbot again, "is beyond your power. Be on your guard lest, having been exalted, you fall. I, on the contrary, order you to serve the brethren, and you will receive a crown from God for your obedience."

Nicetas, drawn by the strongest zeal for the life of reclusion, had not the least desire to attend to what the Abbot said to him. He carried out what he had set his mind on. He shut himself up in reclusion and continued praying without ever going out. After some time, once when he was praying he heard a voice praying with him, and he smelled an extraordinary fragrance. Deceived by this, he said to himself, "If this were not an angel, he would not have prayed with me and there would not have been the fragrance of the Holy Spirit." Nicetas began to pray earnestly, saying, "Lord, manifest Thyself to me intelligibly, that I may see Thee."

Then, there was a voice which said to him, "I will not appear to thee because thou art young, lest, having been lifted up, thou fallest down."

The recluse replied with tears, "Lord, I will never be deluded, because the Abbot taught me not to attend to diabolic delusion, but I will do all that Thou orderest me."

Then, having obtained power over him, the soul-destroying snake said, "It is impossible for a man while still in the flesh to see me. But look, I am sending my angel to stay with thee. Carry out his will."

With these words a demon in the form of an angel

appeared to the recluse. Nicetas fell at his feet and worshipped him as an angel. The demon said, "Henceforth do not pray, but read books. In this way thou wilt enter into constant converse with God and wilt receive the power to give salutary teaching to those who come to thee, and I will unceasingly pray to the Creator of all for thy salvation."

The recluse believed these words and was still further deceived. He stopped praying and occupied himself with reading. He saw the demon constantly praying and rejoiced, supposing that an angel was praying for him. Then he began to talk much from Scripture to those who came to him, and to prophesy like the Palestine recluse.

His fame spread among worldly people and reached the grand prince's court. Actually he did not prophesy, but he told those who came to him where stolen goods had been put or where something had happened in a distant place, obtaining his information from the demon who attended him. Thus he told the Grand Prince Izyaslav about the murder of Prince Gleb of Novgorod, and advised him to send his son to take over the princedom and rule in his stead. This was sufficient for worldly people to hail the recluse as a prophet. It is observable that worldly people and even monks without spiritual discernment are nearly always attracted by humbugs, imposters, hypocrites and those who are in demonic delusion, and they take them for saints and genuine servants of God.

No one could compare with Nicetas for knowledge of the Old Testament. But he could not bear the New

Testament, never took his talks from the Gospels or the Apostolic Epistles, and would not allow any of his visitors to mention anything from the New Testament. From this strange bias in his teaching, the fathers of the Kiev Caves Monastery realized that he was deceived by a demon. At that time there were many holy monks endowed with spiritual gifts and graces in the monastery. They drove the devil from Nicetas by their prayers. Nicetas stopped seeing it. The fathers brought Nicetas out of reclusion and asked him to tell them something out of the Old Testament. But he affirmed with an oath that he never read those books which he previously knew by heart. It turned out that he had even forgotten how to read, so great was the influence of the satanic delusion; and it was only with great difficulty that he learned to read again. Through the prayers of the holy fathers, he was brought to himself, he acknowledged and confessed his sin, he bewailed it with bitter tears, and he obtained a high degree of sanctity and the gift of miracle-working by a humble life among the brethren. Subsequently St. Nicetas was consecrated as Bishop of Novgorod.*

This story raises a question for us today. How can a religious seeker avoid the traps and deceptions which he encounters in his search? There is only one answer to this question: a person must be in the religious search not for the sake of religious *experiences*, which can deceive, but for the sake of *truth*.

---

*Bishop Ignatius Brianchaninov, *The Arena* (Jordanville, New York: Holy Trinity Monastery, 1983), pp. 31–34.

Anyone who studies religion seriously comes up against this question: it is a question literally of life and death.

Our Orthodox Christian Faith, as contrasted with the Western confessions, is often called "mystical": it is in contact with a spiritual reality that produces results which are usually called "supernatural"—which are beyond any kind of earthly logic or experience. One does not need to search in ancient literature to find examples, for the life of a miracle-worker in our own days is full of mystical elements. Archbishop John Maximovitch, who died just fifteen years ago and lived in this very part of California as Archbishop of San Francisco, was seen in glowing light, levitated during prayer, was clairvoyant, worked miracles of healing…. None of this, however, is remarkable in itself; it can easily be imitated by false miracle-workers. How do we know that he was in contact with truth?

2. REVELATION

If you look at a textbook of Orthodox theology, you will find that the truth cannot be found by the unaided powers of man. You can read the Scriptures or any holy book and not even understand what they say. There is an example of this in the Book of Acts, in the story of the Apostle Philip and the Ethiopian eunuch:

> And the angel of the Lord spoke unto Philip, saying, Arise, and go toward the south unto the way that goeth down from Jerusalem unto Gaza, which is desert. And he arose and went: and behold, a man of Ethiopia, a eunuch of great authority under Candace queen of the Ethiopians, who had the charge of all her treasure, and had come to Jerusalem for to worship, was returning,

and sitting in his chariot read Isaiah the prophet. Then the Spirit said unto Philip, Go near, and join thyself to this chariot. And Philip ran thither to him, and heard him read the prophet Isaiah, and said, Understandest thou what thou readest? And he said, How can I, except some man should guide me? And he desired Philip that he would come up and sit with him. The place in the Scripture which he read was this: He was led as a sheep to the slaughter, and like a lamb dumb before his shearer, so opened he not his mouth. In his humiliation his judgement was taken away, and who shall declare his generation? For his life is taken from the earth. And the eunuch answered Philip, and said, I pray thee, of whom speaketh the prophet this? Of himself, or of some other man? Then Philip opened his mouth, and began at the same Scripture, and preached unto him Jesus. And as they went on their way, they came unto a certain water: and the eunuch said, See, here is water; what doth hinder me to be baptized? And Philip said, If thou believest with all thine heart, thou mayest. And he answered and said, I believe that Jesus Christ is the Son of God. And he commanded the chariot to stand still: and they went down both into the water, both Philip and the eunuch; and he baptized him. And when they were come up out of the water, the Spirit of the Lord caught away Philip, that the eunuch saw him no more: and he went on his way rejoicing.

—Acts 8:26–39

There are several supernatural, mystical elements in this account: the angel tells Philip where to go (although to the

Ethiopian it seems like just a chance encounter on a desert road), and later on, after the baptism, the Spirit of the Lord takes up Philip, who disappears before the eyes of the eunuch. But this is not what made the eunuch want to be baptized and become a Christian. There was something else that affected him: not the miracles, but something in his heart. Miracles, although they sometimes help a person to come to faith, are not the right reason to accept Christianity. In the same Book of Acts we read the story of Simon the Sorcerer, who wished to pay money to join the Church and gain the gifts of the Holy Spirit, because they were very spectacular and miraculous. He was in the very lucrative "profession" of sorcery, at a time when the more supernatural things one could do, the more money and prestige one would get, and when there were more of these things happening in Christianity than in the pagan world. As we know from the Book of Acts, Simon's request was denied by the Apostle Peter and he came to a bad end, giving us the word "simony" for the concept of trying to buy the grace of God.

By contrast, when Philip spoke to the Ethiopian eunuch, something in the eunuch's heart changed. It says in the Acts that he came to "believe"; that is, his heart was melted by the truth he heard. The words of Scripture are very powerful, and when the right interpretation is given to them, something in a human being "opens up" if his heart is ready. Therefore, the eunuch accepted Christ with his whole soul; he was a changed man. This was not for the sake of miracles, but for the sake of that which Christ came to earth to bring.

The same thing can be seen in another place of the New Testament, when two of the disciples of Christ were walking on the road to Emmaus (Luke, ch. 24). Christ Himself, on the very day of His resurrection, joined them and began walking

Fr. Seraphim at the St. Herman of Alaska Monastery, at about the time he lectured for the Santa Cruz university students.

Photograph by Mary Mansur.

with them, asking them why they were so excited. They in turn began asking Him if He was the only one who did not know what had happened in Jerusalem. They said that there was a great prophet who had been killed and then had allegedly risen from the dead; but they did not know what to believe. Christ then began to open their hearts and to explain what the Old Testament said was going to happen to the Messiah. All this time the disciples did not recognize Him, for He did not come to them with signs and wonders to dazzle them. Later on, when they came to Emmaus, Christ made as though He would have gone further, and He would have departed from them unrecognized had they not asked Him—out of simple love for a stranger in need—to spend the night with them. Finally, when He sat down with them and "broke the bread" as He had done at the Last Supper, their eyes were opened, they saw that it was Christ Himself, and then He vanished right before their eyes. They began to question themselves and remembered that, all the time He had been with them walking on the road, they had had a burning in their hearts, even though they had not recognized Him. What made them recognize Christ in the end was this "burning heart," and not just the fact that He vanished out of their sight, because magicians can do that also. Therefore, it is not first of all miracles which reveal God to men, but something about God that is revealed to a heart that is ready for it. This is what is meant by a "burning heart," by which the two disciples had contact with God Who came in the flesh.

Here we see how what is called "revelation" comes about: the heart is moved and changed by the presence of God, or by someone who is filled with His Spirit, or by just hearing the truth about Him preached. That is also how the Apostles had the power to go out to virtually the whole inhabited earth—to

India (and perhaps even as far as China), to Russia in the north where the Scythians were living, to Britain in the west, and Abyssinia in the south—in order to preach the Gospel to all peoples within the first decades after the resurrection of Christ.

It is the same today, even though people have become much more insensitive and dense spiritually, much less simple, and do not respond as easily to the truth. In the case of Archbishop John, those who have come to believe through him have been moved not first of all by his miracles, but by something that moved their hearts about him. I'll give an example from his life, an incident that occurred in Shanghai, where he was bishop during World War II. It was related to us by a good friend of ours who died a few years ago, a voice instructor named Anna. As she explained it, Archbishop John's fasting was so strict that his lower jaw lost power during fast periods and he spoke very indistinctly. She had the assignment of giving him lessons to exercise his jaw and make him speak a little more clearly. He would always come to her at regular intervals, and when he finished each lesson it was his custom to leave a twenty-dollar American bill. During the war time, this woman was wounded and was dying in a French hospital in Shanghai. It was late at night; there was a fierce storm outside, and no communications were possible in the city. But she had in her heart only one idea. Having been told by the doctors that she was going to die, her only hope was that Archbishop John would come, give her Holy Communion and somehow save her. She begged people to get word to him, but they said it was out of the question. The phones weren't working because of the storm, and the hospital (since it was war time) was locked up for the night. So all she could do was to cry out: "Help! Archbishop John, come!" Of course, people said that the poor

St. John (Maximovitch) of Shanghai and San Francisco
(1896–1966).

woman was raving, for there was no possible contact with him. But that night, as she was shouting these words, the doors opened up in the midst of the storm and in walked Archbishop John, with Holy Communion. He came up to her, gave her Confession, calmed her down (she was, of course, overjoyed), gave her Holy Communion, and left.

The woman slept eighteen hours after this and, waking up the next day, she felt that she had recovered. "It must be the fact that Archbishop John came," she said. "What Archbishop John?" the nurses asked, saying that he couldn't have possibly entered the locked hospital on such a night. The person in the bed next to her said that someone had in fact been there, but still no one believed her. She began to wonder whether she had been having hallucinations. But as the nurses were making her bed that day, they discovered under her pillow a twenty-dollar American bill. "Aha," she said, "that's the proof he was here!"

How, one may ask, did Archbishop John know? How did he manage to get to her, when there was no human communication possible to get the message across to him? One can say that it was revealed to him, because so many things like that were revealed to him. But *how* was it revealed? Why to him and not to someone else? Why is the truth, it would seem, revealed to some and not to others? Is there a special organ for receiving revelation from God? Yes, in a certain sense there is such an organ, though usually we close it and do not let it open up: God's revelation is given to something called a loving heart. We know from the Scriptures that God is love; Christianity is the religion of love. (You may look at the failures, see people who call themselves Christians and are not, and say there is no love there; but Christianity is indeed the religion of love when it is successful and practiced in the right way.) Our Lord Jesus Christ Himself says that it is above all by their *love* that His true disciples are to be distinguished (cf. John 13:35).

If you ask anyone who knew Archbishop John what it was that drew people to him—and still draws people who never knew him—the answer is always the same: he was overflowing with love; he sacrificed himself for his fellow men out of absolutely unselfish love for God and for them. This is why things were revealed to him which could not get through to other people and which he never could have known by natural means. He himself taught that, for all the "mysticism" of our Orthodox Church that is found in the Lives of Saints and the writings of the Holy Fathers, the truly Orthodox person always has both feet firmly on the ground, facing whatever situation is right in front of him. It is in accepting given situations, which requires a loving heart, that one encounters God. This loving heart is why anyone comes to a knowledge of the truth, even though God sometimes has to break down and humble a heart to make it receptive—as in the case of the Apostle Paul, who at one time was breathing fire against and persecuting Christians. But to God, the past, present and future of the human heart are all present, and He sees where He can break through and communicate.

The opposite of a loving heart that receives revelation from God is cold calculation, getting what you can out of people; in religious life, this produces fakery and charlatanism of all descriptions. If you look at the religious world today, you see that a great deal of this is going on: so much fakery, posing, calculation, so much taking advantage of the winds of fashion which bring first one religion or religious attitude into fashion, then another. To find the truth, you have to look deeper.

3. SUFFERING

A year or so ago I had a long talk on a train ride with a young American. He met me seemingly by chance (of course, there is no chance in life) and told me that he was learning Russian. He was a religious seeker who had been to all kinds of so-called Christian groups, had found nothing but hypocrisy and fakery everywhere and had been ready to give up on religion altogether. But then he heard that in Russia people were suffering for their faith. Where there is suffering, he thought, there will probably be something real, and there will not be such fakery as we have in America. And so he was studying Russian with the purpose of going to Russia and meeting people who were real Christians. As a Russian Orthodox priest, I was astonished to hear this, for he had never before seen an Orthodox pastor nor attended any Orthodox service. We had a long discussion about religion, and I saw that his idea was quite sound: the idea that *suffering* might produce something genuine, while our indulgent life easily produces fakery.

In the fourth century, a great Orthodox theologian, St. Gregory of Nazianzus (also called "the Theologian") described our religion as "suffering Orthodoxy"—and so it has been from the beginning, throughout the whole history of the Church. The followers of the crucified God have suffered persecution and tortures. Almost all the apostles died as martyrs, Peter being crucified upside down, and Andrew being crucified on an x-shaped cross. During the first three centuries of Christianity, believers fled to the catacombs and endured tremendous sufferings. It was in the catacombs that the

29

Church's Divine services—which we celebrate today in a form little changed since that time—were worked out in an atmosphere of constant expectation of death. After the age of the catacombs there was the struggle to retain the purity of the Faith, when many teachers tried to substitute personal opinions for the Divinely revealed teachings given by our Lord Jesus Christ. In later centuries, there were the invasions of Orthodox countries by Arabs, Turks, other non-Christian peoples, and finally—in our own days—by Communists. Communism, which has persecuted religion as it has never been persecuted before, has attacked first of all precisely the Orthodox lands of Eastern Europe. As can be seen, therefore, our Faith actually is a *suffering* Faith; and in this suffering, something goes on which helps the heart to receive God's revelation.

What does the suffering Orthodoxy of Russia—the suffering religion that the above-mentioned young man wanted to see—have to say to us today? Is the truth being revealed in Russia to loving hearts? According to worldly logic, there should be no chance of this. Communism has reigned with an iron hand for over sixty years, and from the very beginning its idea has been to "stamp out" religion. For a time, in the late 1930s, it almost succeeded in this aim, leaving very few churches open. Unless Hitler's invasion had required the Russian people to become patriotic and have some hope in life besides that of Communist ideology, the Church could have been driven entirely underground. Today the situation is somewhat better, but still there is a great deal of pressure upon believers. There was a renewed persecution in the 1960s under Khrushchev, which resulted in about three-fourths of the then-open churches being closed. At the present time, apart from the cities where tourists go (in Moscow or Leningrad, for example, you'll see perhaps thirty or forty churches open), there are large cities in the provinces with few or no churches. Thus, if a believer wants his child to be baptized, he will sometimes have to travel hundreds of miles.

Here I would like to say a word about how God is revealing Himself to the suffering Christians in Russia right now. Probably all of you have heard of Alexander Solzhenitsyn, a great Russian novelist and thinker who was exiled from his native land in 1975 for speaking the truth about Russia as he saw it. His age is almost exactly the same as the age of the Communist regime itself, so he cannot be accused of having prejudices left over from his childhood. He lived a typical life in the Soviet Union. Born one year after the Revolution, he lost his father in World War I, studied mathematics in order to get a practical job, served as a soldier in World War II and went with the Soviet army to Germany. In 1945 he was arrested for writing disrespectful remarks about the "moustache" (meaning Stalin) in private letters, and received eight years in a concentration camp. At the end of this sentence, in 1953, he was exiled (which means he was not exactly in prison, but neither was he free to go anywhere) to a city in southern Kazakhstan, at the edge of the desert. There he contracted cancer and nearly died from it, but was healed in a cancer clinic (about which he wrote a novel, *Cancer Ward*). In this place of exile he taught math and physics, and in secret wrote novels and stories. After Stalin died there was a temporary era of "thaw" or "softening," and he was allowed to be free and publish one book in Russia, in 1961. It was then discovered that he was more "dissident" than the Communist government liked, and he was not allowed to publish anything else. His novels, however, began to be published outside of Russia. This made him a very troublesome celebrity for the Soviet authorities, especially when he received the Nobel Prize in 1970 and was not allowed to receive it in person. In 1975 he was finally forcibly exiled, being given a few days' notice and sent to West Germany.

Solzhenitsyn now lives in Vermont, where he continues his writing. He has been speaking to the West about something very important: the meaning of the atheist experiment in Russia. He looks at this experiment not primarily from a political point of view, but from a more down-to-earth and even spiritual perspective. In a way, he is a symbol of the contemporary Orthodox revival in Russia, because he has undergone the more than sixty years of suffering of the Russian people, and has come out undefeated by it. He has a very strong Christian faith, and a message to the world based upon his experience. His monumental book *The Gulag Archipelago* should be read by anyone who wishes to understand atheism as it has been practiced in Russia and what it does to the human soul.

Solzhenitsyn is not bitter about his experiences in the prison camp and so forth: he emerged a victor over it because he obtained Christian faith. He sees that the system of atheism is not just something Russian, but a universal category of the human soul. Once you have the idea that atheism is true and there is no God, then—as Dostoyevsky wrote in his novels—everything becomes permitted: it becomes possible to experiment with anything that comes to you, any new inspiration, any new way of looking at things, any new kind of society.

Solzhenitsyn's value is that he shows that, once atheism becomes the dominant philosophy and the idea is present that all

Alexander Solzhenitsyn lecturing at Harvard University in 1976.

religion must be exterminated (which is the center of Communist ideology), then there must be prison camps. Man wants religion, and if it is forbidden, he must be somehow gotten rid of. Therefore, since atheism is based on the evil in man's nature, the "Gulag" prison system is the natural expression of the atheist experiment in Russia.

This, however, is a secondary point. The main thing I would like to talk about is what happened to Solzhenitsyn (in the religious sense) when he went to prison, for it was there that God was revealed to him. At the same time that the Gulag reveals the evil in man's nature, it is also the starting point for a man's spiritual rebirth. This is what makes the spiritual rebirth that is now occurring in Russia much more profound than the various "spiritual revivals" which are occurring in the free world. Solzhenitsyn himself says the following about how he came to faith: "It was granted me to carry away from my prison years on my beaten back, which nearly broke beneath its load, this essential experience: *how* a human being becomes evil and *how* he becomes good. In the intoxication of youthful successes I had felt myself to be infallible, and I was therefore cruel." (He was a sergeant in the army.) "In the surfeit of power I was a murderer and an oppressor. In my most evil moments I was convinced that I was doing good, and I was well supplied with systematic arguments. And it was only when I lay there on rotting prison straw that I sensed within myself the first strivings of good."

Here his heart begins to become soft and receptive, and thus a kind of revelation takes place: "Gradually, it was disclosed to me that the line separating good and evil passes not through states, nor between classes, nor between political parties—but right through every human heart—and then through all human hearts.... And even within hearts overwhelmed by evil, one small bridgehead of good is retained. And even in the best of all hearts, there remains ... an unuprooted small corner of evil."*

How much deeper is this observation than anything we in the West could say based on our own experience. It is deeper because it is based on *suffering*, which is the reality of the human condition and the beginning of true spiritual life. Christ Himself came to a life of suffering and the Cross; and the experience in Russia enables those who undergo it to see this profoundly. That is why the Christian revival in Russia is such a very deep thing.

4. REBIRTH

Now I'd like to say a word about a simpler man by the name of Yuri Mashkov, who gives an account of his conversion in Russia. He was forcibly exiled from Russia three years ago and, when still in his early forties, had cancer and died last year. Just three months after arriving in this country, he gave a talk in which he told how he came to faith: that is, how God was revealed to him through his sufferings. He had been invited to speak at a Russian conference in New Jersey in 1978, and when he came to this talk he told the people that, before coming there, he had not known what he was going to say. "I was disturbed," he said. "It seemed to me that I had nothing to tell you. The first half of my life I was a student, and the second half I spent in prisons and the political concentration camps of the Gulag. Indeed, what can I say to people who are more educated than I, more erudite, and even better informed about events in the Soviet Union?"

* Alexander Solzhenitsyn, *The Gulag Archipelago Two* (New York: Harper and Row, 1975), pp. 615–16.

Here we can see a contrast with what happens in the West. There are, it is true, many people in the West being converted to Orthodoxy. Usually they have a broad theoretical knowledge of Orthodoxy, but not this experience of suffering and having to really "pay for what you get." Yuri, on the other hand, speaks not from books, but from his own experience.

"Therefore," Yuri says, "I decided not to write down my talk, but to say whatever God would place in my soul. And then, as we were hurrying away from Bridgeport, Connecticut, in a splendid automobile along the astonishing freeway in the midst of a luxuriant nature, I understood that all my spiritually tormenting life in the Communist 'paradise,' my path from atheism and Marxism to Orthodox faith ... is the only valuable information that can be of interest to you. My life is of interest only inasmuch as it is a drop in the ocean of the Russian religious rebirth."

Yuri then tells about his life: "I was born in the bloody year of 1937 in the village of Klishev, thirty miles from Moscow.... My father, a blacksmith by profession, died in the war, and I do not remember him; my mother, who worked at various jobs, was, I think, indifferent to religion. My grandmother, it is true, was religious." (In fact, in Russia you will find almost always one grandmother or mother who is religious and who will often bring the family back to faith.) "... But she had no authority in my eyes because she was totally illiterate. Of course I was baptized as a child, but in my school years I took off my cross and until the age of twenty-five was a convinced atheist. After finishing the seven-year (primary) school, I had the good fortune to enter the Moscow Higher School of Art and Industry, and I studied there five years out of the seven. Thus, outwardly my life had begun very successfully.... In time I should have received the diploma of an artist and would be able to work anywhere I wanted."

This is a typical Soviet academic biography. In the Soviet Union, academic life is taken very seriously: if you pass, you get an "open ticket" to many good things in Soviet life, and if you fail you get a job such as cleaning the streets.

"But the boring Soviet life and spiritual dissatisfaction," continues Yuri, "gave me no peace, and somewhere at the end of 1955, in my nineteenth year, there occurred an event, outwardly unnoticeable, which however overturned my life and (finally) brought me here. This event occurred in my soul and consisted in the fact that I *understood* in what kind of society I was living. Despite all the naked Soviet propaganda, I *understood* that I was living under a regime of absolute rightlessness and absolute cruelty. Very many students came to the same conclusion at this time, and in time there appeared those who thought as I did, and we all considered it our duty to tell the people about our discovery and to somehow act against the triumph of evil." (This, of course, reflects the idealistic current of youth, which is to be seen in the Western world also.) "But the secret police very carefully looks after all the citizens of the USSR, and when on November 7, 1958 (when I was just twenty-one years old), we gathered at an organizational meeting to decide the question of an underground publication, six of us were arrested and all who did not repent were given the highest punishment for anti-Soviet agitation—seven years each in concentration camp. Thus began a new path in my life."

Up to here, it should be noted, there is no religious conversion at all. Yuri is still just an idealistic youth who has suddenly been "squashed" and sent away to the Gulag.

"All of us then were atheists and Marxists of the 'Euro-Communist' camp. That is, we believed that Marxism in itself was a true teaching which leads the people to a bright future, to a kingdom of freedom and justice, and the Moscow criminals for some reason did not want to realize this teaching in life. In the concentration camp this idea completely and forever died in all of us."

Here I will not go into the question or philosophy of Communism, but will only note the fact that Yuri was reduced to a state of despair. He lost faith in what he had once believed through his training: that Communism is an idealistic teaching that brings happiness and peace. He saw that, in practice, Communism was not what it was claimed to be. Then something began to happen to his soul.

"I would like to reveal a little the process of spiritual rebirth," he says, "so that you can see how unfailingly it is proceeding in the Russian people. It is not only I and those who were with me who have gone through the spiritual path from atheism to religious faith. This is a typical manifestation for the Soviet political concentration camps. What is happening with our people? The process of spiritual rebirth has two stages. At first we discern the essence of Marxism and are freed from any illusions with regard to it. Under a profound and thoughtful analysis we discover that Marxism in its essence is a complete teaching of totalitarianism, that is, an absolute slavery, and any Communist party in any country, once having undertaken the realization of the Marxist program, will be compelled to repeat what the Moscow Communists have done and are doing, or else renounce Marxism and atheism and liquidate themselves. Having understood this simple truth, we lose the ideological basis on which we had opposed

Marxist slavery. We fall into a spiritual vacuum which draws after it an ever profounder crisis."

Yuri then tells how he himself began to enter this profound crisis: "After being freed from camp (that is, after the seven-year term), our prospects were such that we could not wish for an enemy: either we would go back to the camp and remain there for the rest of our lives, or we might die in a psychiatric prison, or we might be murdered by the secret police without a trial or investigation.

"In these conditions of spiritual crisis, with no way out, there inevitably comes upon us the chief question of a worldview: what am I living for if there is no way out? And when this frightful moment comes, each of us feels that death has caught him by the throat: if some kind of spiritual answer does not come, life comes to an end, because without God not only is 'everything permitted,' but life itself has no value and no meaning. I saw in the camp how people went out of their minds or ended with suicide. And I myself clearly felt that if, after all, I came to the firm and final conclusion that there is no God, I would simply be obliged to end with suicide, since it is shameful and belittling for a rational creature to drag out a senseless and tormenting life. Thus, at the second stage of spiritual rebirth we discover that atheism, thought out to its logical end, inevitably brings a man to perdition, because it is a complete teaching of immorality, evil and death.

"A tragic end (suicide or madness) would have been my lot too if, to my good fortune, there had not occurred, on September 1, 1962, the greatest miracle in my life. No event occurred on that day, there were no suggestions from outside; in solitude I was reflecting on my problem: 'to be or not to be?' At this time I already realized that to believe in God is a saving thing. I very much wanted to believe in Him; but I could not deceive myself: I had no faith.

"And suddenly there came a second, when somehow for the first time I saw (as if a door had opened from a dark room into the sunny street), and in the next second I already knew for sure that God exists and that God is the Jesus Christ of Orthodoxy, and not some other God. I call this moment the greatest miracle because this precise knowledge came to me not through reason (I know this for sure) but by some other way, and I am unable to explain this moment rationally.... And so by such a miracle my new spiritual life began, which has helped me to endure another thirteen years of life in concentration camps and prisons, a forced emigration, and, I hope, will help me to endure all the difficulties of emigrant life.

"And this 'moment of faith,' this greatest miracle, is being experienced now in Russia by thousands of people, and not only in concentration camps and prisons. Igor Ogurtsov, the founder of the Social-Christian Union, came to faith not in the camps but in the university. Religious rebirth is a typical phenomenon of contemporary Russia. Everything spiritually alive inevitably returns to God. And it is absolutely evident that such a saving miracle, despite the whole might of Communist politics, can be performed only by the Almighty God, Who has not left the Russian people in terrible sufferings and totally defenseless before many enemies."*

5. CONCLUSION

The experience of this one man, Yuri Mashkov, shows us in a most practical way how God reveals Himself. Something

* *La Renaissance Russe,* 1978, no. 4, pp. 12–17.

happens in the heart; and, while suffering helps this transformation, there is no infallible means of achieving it. For example, much literature has come out of Russia in the last sixty years describing cases of suffering people who have *not* converted. There is a very interesting book in English by a Russian named Marchenko, called *My Testimony.** Marchenko is simply an honest man who could not stand the frightful feeling of fakery in Soviet Russia—the fact that everyone lies to you. Therefore he told the truth, and in doing this he was sent to the camps. The authorities subjected him to the usual interrogations and kept telling him: "You know, if you keep your ideas, even if you get out you're going to come back here. Why don't you just change and do what everyone else does?" "I can't," he said, "I'm an honest man!" Looking at believers, he concluded that they were the only happy people in the prison camps, since they say, "I'm suffering for Christ," and accept what comes to them. "But I can't be like them," he said, "because I don't believe in Christ." And so he just got mad, looked at the jailers and wanted to pound the doors at them. When he got out of prison, he was filled with bitterness and wanted to kill off all his oppressors. He knew that he would just go back to the camp; and, in fact, after he wrote his book he was sent back again.

Thus we see that, in Marchenko's case, so far the heart did not melt, but remained hard. Of course, the heart is a very complex thing, and maybe someday he *will* change. His testimony, however, shows that we cannot simply put a man into prison camp and say, "We'll make him a Christian this way." Some become Christian and some do not. When conversion

---

* Anatoly Marchenko, *My Testimony* (New York: E. P. Dutton & Company, 1969).

does take place, the process of revelation occurs in a very simple way; a person is in need, he suffers, and then somehow the other world opens up. The more you are in suffering and difficulties and are "desperate" for God, the more He is going to come to your aid, reveal Who He is and show you the way to get out.

This is why it is not spectacular things like miracles that we should look for. We know from the story of St. Nicetas related earlier that this is the worst possible approach and leads to deception. The right approach is found in the heart which tries to humble itself and simply knows that it is suffering, and that there somehow exists a higher truth which not only can help this suffering, but can bring it into a totally different dimension. This passing from suffering to transcendent reality reflects the life of Christ, Who went to His suffering on the Cross, endured the most horrible and shameful type of death, and then, totally to the consternation of His own disciples, rose from the dead, ascended into heaven, sent His Holy Spirit and began the whole history of His Church.

That is basically what I wanted to say about revelation in Orthodoxy. You can ask some questions or have discussion on this topic.

6. QUESTIONS AND ANSWERS

Q: If the demons appear as angels and say the things angels would say, then how can one distinguish what is the truth?

A: That's a very good question. You have to be humbling yourself; you have to be in a state of wanting the truth of God and not seeking after "experiences." Of course, I would say to become an Orthodox Christian and find out the whole discipline of leading a Christian life. This helps, though it is no guarantee because you can be deceived as an Orthodox Christian, too.

The Church Fathers give basic words of advice. For example, they say that, if someone appears to you as an angel of light, distrust it. God will not condemn you if He actually wants to appear to you and you reject Him, because if He really wants to get a message across He'll come again and find a way of getting through to you. In fact, He praises you for being distrustful because you don't want to fall into deception.

Those who are in a more advanced spiritual state, with more experience in these things, have acted in other ways. We have an example from the life of St. Anthony the Great, who was all the time seeing demons. When he was asked how he could distinguish the spirits, he said, "When an angel appears, I feel very calm, and when a demon appears, even if he looks like an angel, I feel a disturbance." This, however, is a very dangerous approach for beginners, because you can also feel very calm about demons if you aren't experienced.

The basic answer to your question is, again, to enter into the discipline of the Orthodox Church. As you read accounts such as that of St. Nicetas and see how demons manifest themselves, you can often, just by knowing a typical way by which they will try to trick you, instantly refuse a deception.

Q: Could you talk about the Orthodox view of the Holy Spirit and, in relation to that, the view on non-Orthodox Christian sacraments—whether the Holy Spirit is present in them?

A: The Holy Spirit was sent by our Lord Jesus Christ on the day of Pentecost, the fiftieth day after His resurrection, the tenth day after He Himself ascended to heaven, in order to remain with the Church to the end of time. Historically, there was one Church which He founded.

There are cases in modern times where people have looked historically to find this Church. For example, there is the whole history of the Church in Uganda. In the 1920s, two seminarians from Uganda were studying in an Anglican seminary and began to see that the teaching they were being given was not the same as the teaching they were reading in the ancient Fathers. They then began to think that Roman Catholicism must be the answer—that that must be the ancient Church. In their "search for the true, ancient Church" (as they called it), they went to study in a Roman Catholic seminary and saw that, again, the teaching they received there was different from that of the ancient Fathers of the Church. They began to say, "If the truth can be changed like that, then where is the truth of Christ?" And then they heard about the Orthodox Faith and went through all kinds of trials to find where it was. They first found someone who called himself Orthodox but was just a charlatan, giving out what he called sacraments. When a Greek layman told them that there was something "funny" about that man, they saw this, repented, changed their minds and began to search again. The first Orthodox bishop they encountered was not a very good bishop, and he said, "Oh, don't bother. All religions are the same; go back to the Anglicans." And they didn't let *that* discourage them. Finally they found an Orthodox bishop who was teaching what he should be teaching, and they became Orthodox. Today the Church is spreading in Africa: throughout Uganda, Kenya, Zaire, Tanzania, and so forth. We even have recordings of their services, which are very impressive. They have taken Byzantine, Greek chant and, without their trying to do anything to it (they simply chant in their own way, in their own language), it comes out sounding very dignified, with a kind of local African flavor. They did to the Byzantine chant the same thing that the Greeks did when they took the Hebrew chant.

So these Africans looked historically and found that there is one Church that comes down directly from Christ and teaches what was taught in ancient times: the Orthodox Church. From a historical perspective, you can also see that the other churches have deviated from this: Roman Catholicism first of all in the eleventh century, when the issue finally came to a head about the position of the Pope in the Church, and the Pope rejected the Orthodox answer, taking the whole West with him.

To this day, the Holy Spirit acts in the Orthodox Church. In most Western, Protestant groups, whatever they have are seldom even called sacraments, and so you wouldn't really look for the grace of the Holy Spirit in something which they themselves don't regard as sacraments. Of course, Roman Catholics and a few other groups *do* consider themselves to have sacraments. I myself would say that the true sacraments, in the sense that Christ founded them, are to be found only in the Orthodox Church; and those who, taking the name of sacrament, try to make the best they can out of it—that's a matter between the soul and God, and whatever God may want to do with that soul—that's His affair. It might not be only a psychological thing; I don't know—that's for God to choose. But the means He instituted in the Church have come down to this very day in the Orthodox Church. In fact, you can see historically that we do the same things that were done in the ancient Church. Philip, for example, took the eunuch into the river and baptized him in undoubtedly the very same way that we do: the three immersions in the Name of the Father, the Son, and the Holy Spirit. That is why Orthodoxy is known for being so "old-fashioned": we deliberately keep the old-fashioned ways that came down from Christ, the Apostles, and the early Fathers of the Church.

Q: Would you speak about the Orthodox attitude towards non-Christian religions?

A: Christ came to enlighten mankind. There are various religions outside His revelation where the followers are sincere—not just practicing demon worship—and where the soul is really trying to get through to God. I would say that, before the people have heard of Christ, these religions are fine as far as they go, but they will not get you to the goal. The goal is eternal life and the Kingdom of Heaven, and God came in the flesh to open this up to us. Therefore, Christianity is true; you can point to the various comparative elements of truth in other religions and often they are very profound, but they do not open up heaven. Only when Christ came to earth and told the thief, "You will be with Me in Paradise," was heaven actually opened up to men.

Q: So, people who haven't had any exposure to Christ don't have access to the truth?

A: Those who have never heard of Christ?—that's for God to judge. In the Old Testament, people never heard of Christ either, and then Christ came and preached to them in hell. And St. John the Baptist also, we believe, came to hell before Christ and preached that Christ was about to come there in order to liberate all those who wanted to be liberated, who wanted to believe in Him. So God can open the truth to those who never had a chance to hear: that is, who did not reject the Gospel but just didn't hear about it. But once you *accept* the revelation, then of course you are much more responsible than anyone else. A person who accepts the revelation of God come in the flesh and then does not live according to it—he is much worse off than any pagan priest or the like.

Q: Something I don't know much about, and probably a lot of other people don't is: what are some of the concrete differences and similarities between, say, the Russian Orthodox Church and, say, the Roman Catholic Church with regard to different doctrines and ideas, like about the Trinity or whether the priests marry or not—all those million and one little differences.

A: There are a lot of little differences. There is one main difference, I think; and I would explain it precisely in connection with the Holy Spirit. The Church of Christ is that which gives grace to people; and in the West, when Rome broke off from this Church, this grace was actually lost (maybe people incidentally found it here and there, but from their whole Church the grace was cut off). I look at modern Roman Catholicism as an attempt to substitute, by human ingenuity, the grace which it lost. Therefore, it makes the Pope "infallible," having to give an answer to the question of "where is truth?"

There are some who look at our Orthodox Church and say, "It's impossible for people to find truth there. You say you don't believe in any one pope or bishop, and thus there is no guarantee; you don't believe in the Scriptures like a Protestant might and say that they are the absolutely 'infallible' word. If you have a controversy, where is the final word?" And we say that the Holy Spirit will reveal Himself. This happens especially when bishops come together in council, but even then there can be a false council. One might then say, "There's no hope!" But we say that the Holy Spirit guides the Church, and therefore He will not be false to the Church. If you haven't got the feeling that this is so, then you devise things like making the Bible infallible, making the Pope infallible. Also, you may make Orthodox things—as the Roman Catholics did—into some kind of "law," so that everything is nicely defined: if you break this law you go to your confessor, get such-and-such a penance, and you're all "set" again. Orthodoxy does not believe this way; from this came the whole idea of indulgences, which is a totally legalistic perversion of the idea of repentance. If you repent, like the thief on the cross, you can be saved at that moment.

Orthodoxy always emphasizes this spiritual aspect of the relationship of one's own soul to God; and all the sacraments and discipline of the Church are only a means of getting one's soul right with God: this is the whole of our Faith. In the Roman Church, until very recently when things began to dissolve, the emphasis was rather on obeying a whole set of laws and thereby getting "right" with God in a legalistic sense, which is a substitute for the Holy Spirit.

Q: Could you say something specifically about Anglicanism, because there is a certain similarity between it and what you said about the Roman Catholics saying the Pope is infallible and the Protestants saying the Bible is infallible. I see Anglicanism in the sense of trying to balance out those two views, although I realize you can say that, historically, it is a break-off from the ancient Church.

48

A: In many cases, Anglicans are trying hard, but they're starting from so far away. When you come to God, you can't just "think it out" or "devise a system": you have to come into living contact with His grace. Therefore, the answer for Anglicanism is to come into contact with the Church.

Q: Does the Orthodox Church still have fasting and all the early traditions with regard to Lent?

A: Yes, there is a definite discipline of fasting, just like in ancient times. This has come down from very early in the history of the Church. We know from *The Didache* (The Teaching of the Twelve Apostles) that in the first century there was fasting on Wednesdays and Fridays.

Q: You gave a talk last night on the Apocalypse. Can you briefly summarize that for us?

A: I was looking at events that are happening today as signs of the end, and what our Christian attitude towards the end should be. We should not be counting the years or calculating who is the "King of the South," the "King of the North," and so on, but going more deeply. All the early Apostles, in their epistles, write about the necessity of thinking Christ is near, for preparing oneself, being first of all spiritually prepared. If we're in this state of expectation of Christ coming in a spiritual sense to us, whether to our own souls through grace or at the time of our own death, then the question of when He is going to come physically to this earth at the end of the world will not upset us to such an extent that we will join some new sect that goes to the top of a mountain and waits for the day to come. The day and the hour we do not know; the main priority is spiritual preparation.

Our times, however, are so filled with what could be called "apocalyptic" events that we should be very aware of them. Our Lord says that, although we do not know the day and the hour, we should take example from the fig tree, which when its leaves become green we know that summer is close. Likewise, when all these things begin to happen—when it becomes possible for there to be one world government, when the Gospel is being preached to all peoples, when so many spiritual currents are coming into being which are obviously deceptive—they are clearly signs that something momentous is about to happen, and are very likely bound up with the end of the world.

In order to be spiritually prepared for this, it is very instructive for us to be reading about what happens to people in prison camps. Such accounts show us that, no matter what might happen—even if we are under Antichrist himself and placed in a prison—we can survive because we have Christ. The lives of martyrs have always been a source of instruction and edification, and even today people are being martyred whom we can learn about.

AFTERWORD

Thus ended Fr. Seraphim's talk. Less than two years later, he was dying in a hospital. In the intense suffering of his final illness, the heavenly realm for which he had long been preparing himself became more near and tangible. God, Who had once fulfilled his tormenting, all-consuming desire for transcendent Truth, now consoled him in unseen ways. Unable to speak, he only gazed up into heaven while tears streamed from his eyes. Once he tried to tell his monastic brother of a revelation he had received in his hour of trial from his reposed spiritual mentor, St. John Maximovitch, but his dying body would not allow him. When, on September 2, 1982, his soul was finally freed from his body, his face became radiant and peaceful, and his mouth naturally formed into a gentle smile. Those who saw him in his coffin bore witness to the quiet joy that awaits those whose hearts are receptive to God's revelation.

Except a corn of wheat fall to the ground and die, it abideth alone: but if it die, it bringeth forth much fruit (John 12:24). In the death of Fr. Seraphim, a seed was planted that has continued to bring forth fruit in the lives of God-seekers. Through the publication of his many books and of his biography (*Father Seraphim Rose: His Life and Works*), he has become known throughout the world as a bridge between uprooted modern man and the fulness of truth. The acquisition of this truth, as he said, requires no exalted states of consciousness, but only a loving heart that is *broken and contrite* (Ps. 50:17), made open to God's revelation through suffering, repentance, and faithful longing. Having received Fr. Seraphim's vital transmission of ancient Christian wisdom, may yet more loving hearts begin to burn for the truth, and may they find it in the Person of the living Christ.

St. Herman Press

ST. HERMAN OF ALASKA BROTHERHOOD

For over four decades, the St. Herman Brotherhood has been publishing works of Orthodox Christian spirituality. Write for our free catalogue, featuring over fifty titles.

St. Herman Press
P. O. Box 70
Platina, CA 96076

Visit our website and order online from:
www.sainthermanpress.com